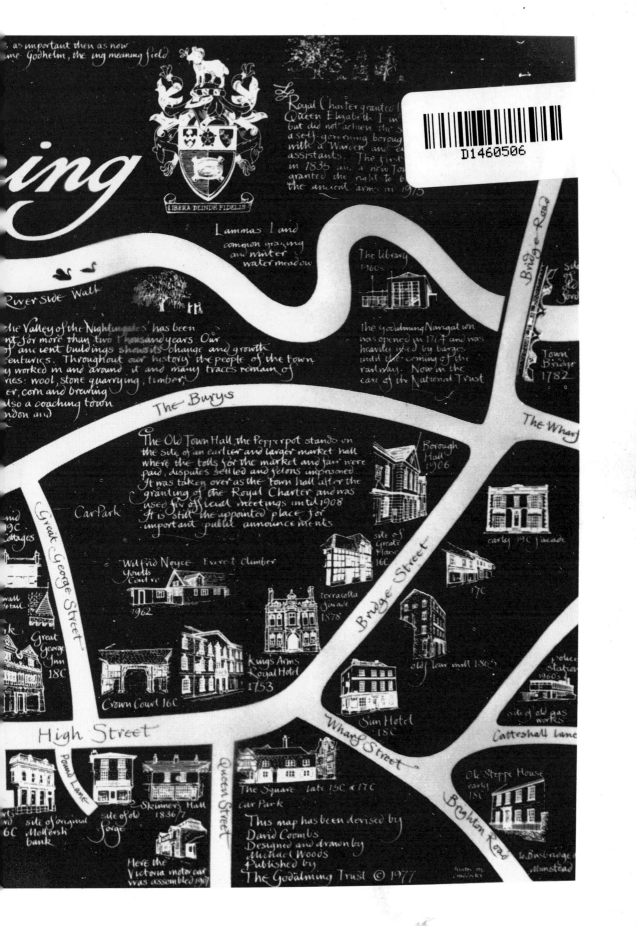

GODALMING
A Pictorial History

Godalming parish church of St Peter and St Paul in 1839, the year before major alterations to the interior to increase the seating capacity and the final westward extension of the nave.

GODALMING
A Pictorial History

Nigel Coates

Phillimore

1995

Published by
PHILLIMORE & CO. LTD.
Shopwyke Manor Barn, Chichester, West Sussex

ISBN 0 85033 983 9

Printed and bound in Great Britain by
BIDDLES LTD.
Guildford, Surrey

I venture to affirm that the possession of beautiful old houses, and of buildings not perhaps beautiful, but of distinct architectural interest, is an important asset, even from the commercial point of view, of such a town as Godalming ... The older buildings, down to the very latest that shows the continuity of architectural progression, are a precious heritage, belonging in a way to the town and the county. To retain them untouched, and to preserve them from decay or demolition, should be felt to be the duty of every good townsman.

Gertrude Jekyll, *Old West Surrey* (1904)

List of Illustrations

Frontispiece: The parish church of St Peter and St Paul

Acknowledgements

Particular thanks are due to Albert Watson for permission to use many of his splendid collection of postcards; to Ron Head for generously undertaking all photographic processing as well as much research work; and to the Trustees of Godalming Museum for the loan of material from the museum archives. I am also grateful to the following for their help in the production of this book: Joan Charman, David Coombs, Alan Bott, John Young, Bob Barnett, Alan High; and to the authors of the various publications listed in the Select Bibliography, to all of which I have turned for reference.

Illustration Acknowledgements

A. Watson, nos. 14-16, 24, 28, 42, 55, 71-74, 76, 77, 81, 88, 92, 97, 99-101, 103-113, 115, 121, 122, 124-126, 133, 134, 145, 148, 149, 151, 153, 154, 166, 167, 171; R. Barnett, nos. 5, 44, 54, 75, 94, 95, 102, 114, 127, 140, 144; R. Head, nos. 3, 9, 56, 85, 130, 152; Godalming Town Council, nos. 41, 160, 161, 163, 170; A. High, no.116; R. Enticknap, no.90; Joseph N. Smith, Atlanta, no.22; David Frith, Editor *Wisden Cricket Monthly*, no.136; University of Reading, Rural History Centre, no.165. All other pictures are reproduced by permission of the Trustees of Godalming Museum.

Introduction

Saxons

On an ancient tomb in Godalming parish church lies a ring of stone, decorated with animals' heads, dating from the ninth century. The present church has grown from a Saxon core of the early 11th century so the stone ring was presumably part of an earlier building. It can be taken as the first tangible piece of the town's history, for before that all is conjecture, perhaps fortunately since it allows historians to postulate a founding father, Godhelm, who led his people to settle in this favoured spot and bequeathed it a name unique in the world.

The site of Godalming must have been known to people for millennia before the Saxon settlement. It lay on a dry shelf at the meeting point of river valleys, sheltered by abrupt cliffs of sandstone whose flat summit could be easily worked by primitive tools. Only two miles to the north ran one of prehistory's greatest arterial trackways, in its time known by many names: North Downs Way, Harrow Way, Pilgrims' Way, the Tin Road. It carried travellers from the Kent coast to Stonehenge and the Wiltshire uplands, on to Cornwall and even further if we are to judge from the fact that two axe-heads made of a dark stone from Ireland have been found near Godalming. Iron-Age forts and Romano-British villas have been excavated at Hascombe, Charterhouse and Binscombe but nothing pre-Saxon has been found on the lower ground. The first Saxons themselves seem to have divided their settlement between the bottom and the top of Holloway Hill, for in the woods at Tuesley they made a shrine to the powerful god Tiw. Assuming their arrival to have been in about A.D. 600 this would have made them contemporaries of Augustine's Christian missionaries who were just starting their work in Kent. Pope Gregory had wisely ordered that temples of heathen sacrifice should be purified, not destroyed, so that people would continue to go to the accustomed place for the new Christian worship; this happened in Godalming, though before long a new church was built where that of St Peter and St Paul now stands above the river. The site of the ancient minster on the hill is now marked by a statue of the Blessed Virgin Mary.

There followed 200 years of work to bring the wild land under control: marshes were drained, trees felled, land ploughed and pigs herded ever further into the fringes of the Weald. During this period, the manor of Godalming took shape, finally stretching from Artington at the foot of the chalk to Haslemere in the south, and by the time of King Alfred it had come into the ownership of the royal house of Wessex. Then for a time there was fear of attack by Danes and this part of England was protected by a network of fortified *burhs*, into which the local population could retreat in time of trouble. In the early 10th century one of these was at Eashing, but it was soon superseded by Guildford. In 1940 the Wey valley was still regarded as a line worth defending, as the few remaining brick and concrete pillboxes bear witness.

Normans

Almost immediately following the death of Alfred in 899, the manor which he bequeathed to his nephew began to be broken up into smaller ones as the later Saxon kings rewarded their followers; after the Conquest all these came under new Norman overlords. The name of Ranulf Flambard which adorns the town's new relief road also appears on a board in the parish church as the second rector of Godalming. Possibly he never came here as he was also Bishop of Durham, Dean of Christchurch, a canon of Salisbury and, most importantly, financial adviser to William Rufus, but he acquired for himself holdings of land round Godalming church and at Tuesley which were merged to form the Rectory Manor. Flambard fell from power on the accession of Henry I but was subsequently pardoned and allowed to retain his Godalming land till his death in 1128, after which it passed to the Dean and Chapter of Salisbury Cathedral. Their successors kept the connection until the land was disposed of by the Ecclesiastical Commissioners in the mid-19th century. Meanwhile the King's Manor was granted to the Bishops of Salisbury by Henry III and eventually bought by Sir George More in 1601, presumably as a fitting adjunct to his fine new house at Loseley which adjoined Farncombe to the north.

Church Street

An observer standing at the bottom of Church Street can look along it to the historic heart of the town. Inside the church nearby is a Norman chancel which, like the base of the tower, was probably built in Flambard's lifetime. On the left is Church House dating from the 16th century with later additions, now used as offices: carefully maintained above the door is the date 1086—Domesday, of course, and a reminder that a substantial house, probably the residence of the Rectory Manor, stood here then. Ahead lies the vista of Church Street with buildings from five centuries jumbled together in total agreement. To the right the terrace of cottages bears the name Deanery Place to confirm the Salisbury connection, and at the top of the street can be seen the Old Town Hall, alias Pepperbox, now more often modernised to Pepperpot. It stands on the site of an earlier market house which itself may have replaced another building, for it is believed that this spot has always been the central point both of the town with its fairs and markets, first permitted in 1300, and earlier still of the Godalming Hundred which needed an accessible meeting place in which to conduct its business. This is the ancient core of the town where more than a thousand years of history, civic and religious, can be sensed at either end of the street.

Middle Ages

Medieval Godalming prospered, thanks to sensible use of its own natural resources, one of which was the remarkable little stream known as the Ock, a name believed to be derived from a Celtic word for water. It flows through the town to join the Wey, slipping under the Ockford Road and Mill Lane unnoticed by many who pass by. In its powerful youth, during the inter-glacial periods, it was strong enough to cut a deep pass through the sandstone which is now used by road and railway to connect the Wey valley with the open land to the south. Until recently it was noted for its crayfish, a sure indication of pure water, and the certainty of its flow is shown by the fact that at one time it was driving four mills, though not without the aid of a pond in each case. In Mill Lane, Hatch Mill, parts of which date from the 17th century, probably stands on the site of one of the three Godalming mills listed in the Domesday survey.

It was still operating in the Second World War after its overshot wheel had been replaced by modern machinery, but since 1950 it has been used for storage and offices with a car park occupying the site of the former mill pond.

Wool

In contrast to the heavy soil and thick forest of the true Weald, the more open Greensand country, as well as the nearby North Downs, would have been favourable for sheep folding from very early times, and the flocks increased rapidly after the arrival of Cistercian monks at Waverley Abbey in 1128. By the middle of the 13th century fulling mills began to make their appearance and Godalming found itself happily placed for cloth manufacture with abundant supplies of the raw material and water power for processing it; also, not too far way near Redhill were large deposits of fullers earth which was pounded into the cloth to compact it and clean it by absorbing the grease. By 1360 there was a fulling mill working at Catteshall which was taken on by Richard Laneway before the end of the century. His descendants were operators of the mill for the next 200 years, no doubt relieved that they could pay a large part of their rent in eels which filled the traps as they migrated downstream. The family has left its name to posterity in the form of Llanaway, to identify the area between Catteshall and Farncombe. Throughout the next three centuries the woollen industry brought prosperity to Godalming; even as late as 1690 John Aubrey could write, 'This town is eminent for clothing the most of any place in the County'.

Stone

Another piece of good fortune for Godalming can immediately be realised by any visitor to the town: plentiful supplies of good building stone, known as Bargate, dug out of local quarries since pre-Conquest times and used through the centuries in the construction of many buildings—the parish church, Busbridge church, Charterhouse and the splendid walls at the western end of the Burys, for example. It was also used, probably by the monks of Waverley, to build Eashing Bridge, a classic piece of construction which has withstood current and flood for over 600 years. It was the practice in Godalming to open up a new quarry near to where the stone would next be needed and allow the older ones to become overgrown, so there were altogether some 16 excavations round the town of which four were worked till 1939.

Wood

By the late Middle Ages another natural resource, timber, was in great demand both for building and as fuel for the glass and iron industries in the nearby villages, while the growing leather industry required a supply of oak bark, the best though slowest tanning agent. There are early records of concern at the rate of depletion of woodland, also of regulations for coppicing and forest management.

15th Century

The late medieval town had already assumed the main street pattern that we know today; High Street and Church Street contain buildings of this period, though more recent façades may conceal the fact. The secret is brilliantly revealed at the Museum where the original wattle and daub construction has been exposed to view. Further down the High Street the building known as The Square shows how character can be retained through five centuries of alterations; it stands well back from the edge of the street and at one time had a large garden with orchards running up to what are now Brighton Road and Croft Road. Anyone with a sense of history must be thankful that the house was saved from demolition in the recent past to become a doctors' group surgery. Godalming went on its quietly busy way untouched by the dynastic wars of the 15th century. Most of the inhabitants were connected in some way with the woollen industry and the courts of the time seemed to be mainly concerned with fining those who carried on a trade outside the market town or allowed their pigs to stray. The only visible relic of the Wars of the Roses is a tiny replica of the sunburst emblem of the House of York in one of the windows of the parish church.

Tudors

From the Old Town Hall one can look through the arches to see one of the most prominent 16th-century buildings, best known as the *White Hart*, though it started life as the *Antelope*; it still displays the tall archway through which coaches entered the courtyard. In Bridge Street there was another large Tudor building known as The Greate House which was burnt down in 1869, but part of the complex remains having done duty as a brewery malt-house and a builder's premises, now well restored. With such a high proportion of the population working in the wool and leather trades there was a great need for cottage accommodation in the 16th and 17th centuries, and the survivors can be seen all over the town, especially in Mill Lane and Ockford Road. In the 16th century the manor of Godalming reverted to the Crown, which may account for the arms of Henry VIII hanging outside the *King's Arms and Royal Hotel*. During Queen Elizabeth's reign the town moved towards greater independence with the grant of a Wednesday market and a second three-day fair at Candlemas. The culmination of this process was the acquisition of a Charter of Incorporation as a Borough in January 1574 (old calendar) with the right to a common seal but not to a member of Parliament, perhaps because Haslemere already had two. Some years later a further ordinance was made laying down standards of trading and behaviour and adding eight Assistants to help the Warden, who had already contrived to lose the original Charter—the existing version dates from a confirmation issued in 1666. The seal did duty till 1893 when the present coat of arms was devised by the College of Heralds.

17th Century

On the outskirts of Farncombe stand the Wyatt Almshouses, a brick terrace of 10 dwellings and a chapel dated 1622, now surrounded by a modern courtyard. They were built in accordance with the will of Richard Wyatt of Shackleford, a freeman of the Carpenters' Company, to house five poor men of Godalming and five from neighbouring villages. The Master and Wardens of the Company were enjoined to make an annual visit to enquire into the well-being of the occupants, to hear a sermon and then to dine together, a duty which continues to be faithfully carried out. By this time the development of the town was being affected by its proximity to London where fortunes were to be made, and other wealthy figures began to appear. The fashion had been set by Richard Champion of the Drapers' Company, Alderman of the City of London and Mayor there in 1565; another Richard Champion died in 1622 and left money which was merged with a bequest from Henry Smith of Wandsworth, the great Surrey philanthropist, who died in 1627 leaving £1,000 to Godalming and bequests to many other parishes. In our own time this fund is still administered to give financial help to needy people. The advantage of being within a few hours' drive of London worked both ways and at the time of the Civil War the earls of Northumberland and Wimbledon each had a house in Godalming, no doubt finding it less exhausting than life in the capital. The war itself left the town undisturbed; in fact the greatest excitement of the time seems to have been the removal in 1643 of the vicar, Nicholas Andrews, who was accused among other things of being much given to ease and leisure, disapproving of long sermons and frequenting tipplings in inns and taverns. One of the signatories to the Articles of Complaint against the vicar was Phillip Mellersh, High Constable of the hundred and an early representative of one of Godalming's great families.

Oglethorpe

The most famous family arrived in 1688 when the manors of Binscombe and West-brook were bought by Sir Theophilus Oglethorpe, an ardent supporter of the Stuart cause who spent much of the next eight years in France with the exiled James II. He took the oath of loyalty to King William in 1696 and in the same year his ninth child, James Edward, was born. Twenty-five years later the young man succeeded his brother as one of the members of Parliament for Haslemere and immediately began to take an interest in social reform. He continued to live at Westbrook Place, contributing a guinea here and there to good causes, and building a great wall to enclose a fine vineyard; the wall was later fortified by James' sisters during the period of Jacobite plotting in the 1740s, as can be seen today at the house called The Little Fort. Gradually the idea came to Oglethorpe that America must hold out hope for people who, through no fault of their own, needed to make a new start in life. He got together a group of like-minded trustees and applied for a charter to found a colony north of the Spanish settlers in Florida (whom he was later to defeat at the battle of Bloody Marsh). He sailed from Gravesend with about one hundred and twenty emigrants in November 1732, and three months later was starting to lay out the street plan of Savannah, the first town in Georgia. He crossed the Atlantic twice more, and on his final return to England he met and married a rich lady from Essex; they stayed at Westbrook for the honeymoon and then the manor saw little more of its lord for he returned to London, then settled at Cranham with his wife till he died and was buried there in 1785. The great days at Westbrook were over; it passed through a succession of owners before being bought by the Countess of Meath and opened as a home for epileptics which has recently celebrated its centenary—an outcome which would surely have gladdened James Oglethorpe's heart.

Ghosts and Rabbits

At the start of the 18th century Godalming seemed to be going through its silly season. First there was the persistent rumour that James Oglethorpe's elder brother, also called James and reported to have died in infancy, had in fact been substituted for the still-born son of King James II by means of the famous warming pan. The story was retold by servants who had been at Westbrook and given added weight by the fact that the General always refused to reveal his or his brother's dates of birth. Then there was the ghost of Bonny Prince Charlie which many Godalming people claimed to have seen walking under the trees at Westbrook, although there is no record of his ever having stayed there. Most notably there was Mary Tofts whose doctor announced that, having been frightened by rabbits the previous spring, she had now, in November 1726, been delivered of 18 of the little creatures; not surprisingly she made the national press and merited a Hogarth cartoon.

Navigation

In 1782 the Town Bridge, of mellow brick with graceful semi-circular arches, which now links Bridge Street with Bridge Road, was built by George Gwilt to replace the wooden Bishop's bridge which had only been called on to carry traffic in time of flood; it stood beside a ford through the river which was the crossing point of the main road. Probably the ford had become deeper since the construction of the locks and sluice gates of the Godalming Navigation which opened in 1763, linking up at Guildford with the Wey Navigation which had already been operating for over 100 years. The new bridge became the head of navigation on the river and Godalming Wharf, just below, has been the most southerly point of the British inland waterway system since the closure of the Wey-Arun canal in 1871. The immediate urgency was for timber, mostly oak, from the Weald to be transported to the shipyards on the Thames. From London the barges brought back loads of imported timber, corn, wool and rags for making paper. At one time there were 10 barges based at Godalming, and the Wharf was a hive of industry with two timber yards, sheds and stables, and six alehouses in the vicinity, not one of which remains. Barges continued to work sporadically until the 1920s, to be replaced by pleasure craft, many of which now come to Catteshall for refurbishment. The whole Navigation from Godalming to Weybridge is in the care of the National Trust.

Roads

The early days of the Navigation were also the time of the coming of the turnpikes. Most of the roads still kept to the line of the ancient trackways and many had been worn down through soft stone into the hollow ways which some of our country lanes follow so picturesquely today. Toll roads maintained by the turnpike trusts began to be authorised in the late 17th century but the Portsmouth road was not thus upgraded till 1749. This was the road by which all traffic entered Godalming from the north, except for farm wagons which could use the upper ford just below the Boarden footbridge. The track from the Hog's Back through Hurtmore came down the hill through Farncombe to join the Guildford road, giving travellers a first view of the town which has still hardly changed since the 14th century when the church spire first appeared across the meadows. Southward, the road pattern has altered considerably over the centuries. From the top of Holloway Hill both Busbridge Lane and Tuesley Lane ran out into the countryside, the former leading over Hambledon common to Chiddingfold and Petworth until superseded by the present road from Milford in about 1760. Brighton Road did not become a main route to the south until 1826, its name reflecting the increasing popularity and accessibility of the Sussex coast resorts.

Inns

The clue to Godalming's prosperity in the 18th century can be found in Ockford Road where there stands an old milestone nearly opposite the toll house (no. 66); it shows Hyde Park Corner to be 32 miles away, almost the same distance as Portsmouth—an ideal situation for the town's coaching inns. Best known of them was (and still is) the *King's Arms* in the High Street which welcomed the increasing trade with a fine brick façade to replace the one which some 60 years earlier had greeted the Czar of

Russia, Peter the Great, and his retinue returning to London after watching naval exercises. A few years later the nearby *Sun Inn* was rebuilt with some equally pleasing brickwork which today gives such strong character to the curving end of the street. The other inns along the High Street—*Great George, Little George, Angel, White Hart, Red Lion, Richmond Arms*—all thrived on the coach trade, and the town laid on its own coaches to Piccadilly: first the 'Godalming Machine' and then the 'Accommodation', terminating at the *King's Arms*.

Industry

Meanwhile the old industries continued; the tanneries had plenty of work with the increasing demand for harnesses and in fact the tradition was able to continue at Westbrook Mill until about 1950. Thanks to the enterprise of the owner, John Pullman, it was this mill which supplied the power to enable Godalming to become the first town in the world to have electric street lighting, in 1881, though the local gas company soon hit back with a better offer. Godalming was able to retain an interest in textiles thanks to its early adoption of framework knitting, particularly of stockings, both as a cottage industry and in small factories; the last knitwear factory did not close until 1990. Paper making continued at Catteshall Mill, where in 1869 a huge Fourneyron water turbine was installed. Subsequently the mill became an engineering works; the turbine has been removed and is now a scheduled ancient monument.

Victorians

In 1835 the Municipal Corporations Act brought into being the mayor and council; meetings were held upstairs in the new Market House, built on the site of the medieval one in 1814 with money raised by public subscription. The first mayor was Henry Marshall who lived in the house called The Croft in the High Street (now nos. 87-91); his garden ran nearly to the top of Holloway Hill where there was a summerhouse which has now been turned into a tiny residence. All the intervening buildings and Croft Road itself have appeared since that date, for now came the time of the great expansion. From an estimated 2,000 people living in and around Godalming in Tudor times the population had risen only to 3,400 by 1801 but in the next 100 years shot up to over 11,000. There were two pieces of good fortune which guided the development of the town: the Lammas meadows were guarded by the river with its annual floods, and the surrounding hillsides were too steep for houses to be built on them. These physical constraints sent development over the skyline onto the flat hilltops or right over Frith Hill to Farncombe and Binscombe, both of which had been separate hamlets for centuries as their few remaining old buildings can testify. Churches followed the people—to Farncombe with the building of St John the Evangelist in 1847 and to Busbridge 20 years later, both becoming the focal points of new parishes, and the process was to be completed when St Mark's was built in 1934 to serve the needs of residents in the new estates on Ockford Ridge. Although Godalming is visually dominated by its parish church of St Peter and St Paul, there is a strong tradition of nonconformism in the town. John Platt was the head of a weekly conventicle attracting several hundred people to Westbrook Place in the 1660s. In 1665 George Fox, founder of the Quakers, preached at Binscombe where there is a little burial ground used by the Society of Friends until 1790. The Congregational church and school were built at the bottom of Bridge Street in 1868. In 1993 the Godalming Directory listed the churches or meeting places of 12 different Christian denominations.

Railway

The pattern of modern Godalming was set with the coming of the railway. The London and South Western had reached Guildford in 1845 and four years later came to Farncombe, sealing the fate of the barge traffic on the Navigation and of the London coaches. The old station there remained the terminus for 10 years while the line to Portsmouth through Godalming station was being built as a speculation by a contracting company headed by Thomas Brassey who lived for a while at Westbrook Place. He was presumably quite content to see the estate cut off from the town by the railway line which opened in 1859 as a single track link to the coast thanks to a court ruling following the so-called Battle of Havant when London, Brighton and South Coast Railway employees forcibly tried to stop the new line reaching its destination.

Schools

An early result of the coming of the railway was the arrival in 1872 of 153 boys under their headmaster William Haig-Brown to take up residence in the new Bargate stone buildings of Charterhouse, designed by P.C. Hardwick. Within 20 years the number had risen to 500 and the boarding houses were spreading along Frith Hill. A happy relationship was soon established with the school contributing greatly to the cultural and civic life of the town, and making sporting facilities available to the two schools which were already catering for Godalming children—the Bell School on the old workhouse site in Moss Lane and the British School in Bridge Road. In 1885 Ernest Marshall set up a grammar school in the hall at the side of the *Red Lion*.

Authors

Victorian Godalming was well served by a number of local authors all of whom showed a great love for the town. Charles Softley could hardly bring himself to watch the changes that were sweeping over the place he knew so well. 'Now', he wrote, 'from the Burys we recognise little of this past, all obliterated from view—field, hill and bridges vanished, vanished! And hark, the whistling of a train tells the history of the devastation.' Present-day Godhelmians did not invent nostalgia; they treasure their town but would know much less about it were it not for Percy Woods who was born in Brook House, Mint Street, in 1842. He became a senior civil servant but spent his spare time, and all his retirement, in compiling a history of families and properties in the area of the old hundred of Godalming from the 15th to the 19th centuries, amounting to 57 volumes of manuscript, now held in the town museum and available to researchers. Gertrude Jekyll, who lived at Munstead on the outskirts of Godalming and is best known to posterity for her wonderful work with plants and gardens, left a loving portrait of a golden age in her book *Old West Surrey*, remembering the little carts pulled by Newfoundland dogs which brought fish from Littlehampton to Godalming, and telling of the smugglers selling kegs of brandy; they came up from Shoreham to Cranleigh, over Hydon Heath and down into the town by Holloway Hill.

20th Century

Godalming welcomed the 20th century with an outburst of building. Edwin Lutyens had just completed the formidable Red House on Frith Hill, and soon after came Westbrook in splendid Bargate stone built by Hugh Thackeray Turner for his own use. He was responsible for donating much of Milford and Witley commons to the

National Trust, a generous act to be copied in 1952 by Doctor Fox with his gift of Winkworth Arboretum. Also in the first decade of the century the Roman Catholic church appeared in Croft Road, a Methodist church by the river and a Baptist church as well as a fire station in the newly constructed Queen Street, while municipal buildings were erected in Bridge Street, threatening the Old Town Hall with redundancy. In 1912 the town, like the whole country, was shocked to learn of the sinking of the *Titanic*. Her chief wireless operator, Jack Phillips, who died a hero's death, was brought up in Farncombe, and Hugh Thackeray Turner was asked to design a cloister in his memory which was built near the river on the site of the old Rectory Manor pound. Gertrude Jekyll designed the surrounding garden and the memorial was opened just four months before the outbreak of the Great War which was to claim the lives of 105 more Godhelmians whose names are recorded in the parish church. The tragic theme continued with the death of George Mallory during the 1924 Everest expedition; he was a master at Charterhouse, married to the daughter of Thackeray Turner. From the same school, as both a pupil and a master, came Wilfrid Noyce who was a member of the successful Everest team in 1953; he died in the Himalayas in 1962, a few weeks after opening the Godalming Youth Centre which now bears his name.

Houses and Cars

Between the wars, house building went on apace with Council estates appearing at Pondfield in Farncombe and around Binscombe Lane in the '20s, and on Ockford Ridge a little later. The process of infilling in residential areas meant that the old spacious gardens began to disappear. On the other hand, successive governments' Green Belt policies ensured that the countryside around Godalming remained relatively unspoilt. Much of the rest of the 20th century story seems to have revolved round the motor car: as well as the introduction of a 10 m.p.h. speed limit, schemes to cope with its demands have included demolition of the Pepperpot, a bypass across the Lammas lands and a three-lane ring road breaking through Church Street and Mill Lane, all successfully resisted by enraged townsfolk. This book ends with the start of a second Elizabethan age, but there are already new chapters to be written telling of the growing friendship with the twin towns of Mayen in Germany and Joigny in France, the links with Georgia, U.S.A., the building of the High Street relief road and the enhancement of the town centre to make it more attractive to pedestrians. The Borough of Godalming ceased to exist on the eve of its 400th anniversary: most of its powers were taken over by Waverley District (now Borough) Council, but the town remains, and reminders of its long history are all around.

1   The town of Godalming, seen here in about 1914, has
spread along the sandstone shelf above the level of the
Wey flood-plain, protected by the steep slope of Holloway
Hill. The centre of the Saxon settlement of the early 7th
century is believed to have been on the rising ground
beyond the parish church in this picture.

2   'Free and therefore faithful'. The Godalming coat of
arms was granted in 1893. It shows the woolsack, taken
from the old Borough Seal, and a ram, reminders of the
town's early source of wealth. The Tudor rose refers to
the charter of 1575 and the pears make a pun on the
name of John Perrior, first Warden. The dexter shield
relates to early Lords of the Manor.

3 The statue of the Blessed Virgin was erected in the mid-20th century by the sisters of Ladywell Convent to mark the site of the first place of Christian worship in Godalming, at Tuesley. The foundations of a Saxon chapel were unearthed a hundred years earlier. Christians of many denominations gather here for a service at sunrise every Easter Day.

4 Saxon stones dated by the British Museum c.820-840, now in the south chapel of the parish church. Behind is the 13th-century piscina. The stones rest on the Westbrook tomb of 1513.

5 The medieval bridge over the River Wey at Eashing was probably built by the monks of Waverley Abbey. It can still carry modern traffic and is in the care of the National Trust.

6 In 1976 the plaster on this house in Deanery Place opposite the parish church collapsed, revealing briefly the late-medieval timber framing of the original building.

Godalming Church

7 On the right in this 1920s photograph is one of Godalming's finest buildings, Church House, dating back to the 15th century with many subsequent alterations. It was a private house when the picture was taken but has now been converted to offices.

8 Dating from about 1500, The Square was the last private house in the High Street. As such it belonged to the Misses Caswall, nieces of the Victorian hymn-writer of that name. They bequeathed the property to the Borough Council to be used for the benefit of the people of Godalming and it is now a doctors' surgery.

9 This great oak opposite St Mark's school is at least 400 years old with a girth of 18 ft. One wonders how it escaped the axe through the centuries. The plot of land on which it stands was presented to the Borough as a public open space by Mr. W. Hoptroff, one of the builders of the Ockford Ridge estate, in 1935.

10 No.1, Church Street, in late Victorian days. The house is 16th-century but records of a building here called *At Pleystowe* go back to the early 14th century. In 1902 the plaster, seen here, cracked and was removed, revealing a most attractive timbered front which is a prominent feature of the street today. The Mellersh family were solicitors and bankers as well as land agents, and Scriven ran a plumbing business.

11 This is the same house, No.1, Church Street, photographed a few years after the plaster was removed.

12 Sixteenth-century cottages in a most attractive mixture of building materials. This area was for centuries the industrial heart of Godalming until modern factories began to be built along Catteshall Lane. The little bridge carries Mill Lane over the Ock.

13 The Greate House, pictured here shortly before it burned down in 1869, was part of a fine complex of Tudor buildings which dominated Bridge Street, formerly known as Water Lane. The Borough Hall now stands on the lower part of the site.

Godalming. The White Hart.

14 (*above*) Known as *The Antelope* before it became *The White Hart*, this building was a coaching inn from 1570 onwards, as can be guessed from the archway on the left. It was altered to shops in 1932 when the ground and first floors were remodelled. The word 'Entire' in this context is a Victorian version of 'Real Ale'.

A PRETTY CORNER, GODALMING.   221352 JV.

15 A 16th-century cottage, formerly known as 'Whitehall', standing at the corner of Mint Street and Mill Lane. The house on the left of the picture has been demolished and replaced by a sensitively designed building which looks as if it has always been there.

16 (*left*) The Ockford Road, with its picturesque 16th-century cottages, is the main route into Godalming from the south. After the opening of the Godalming Navigation, the tollgate was removed to Ockford Road from north of the town, in order not to lose the revenue from wagons bringing timber up to Godalming Wharf.

17 The Wyatt Almshouses on the edge of Farncombe, built in 1622 in accordance with the will of Richard Wyatt, a London merchant who lived at nearby Shackleford. They were to house five poor men of Godalming and five from neighbouring villages.

18 Another view of the Wyatt Almshouses. There is a chapel in the centre of the row and the whole group is now surrounded by a hollow square of council houses. The well-being of the occupants is still the concern of the Master and Wardens of the Carpenters' Company.

19 Fortunately for the amateur historian the builders of the two shops on the left worked the date, 1663, into the ornate brickwork on the front of the first floor. This picture, taken in the 1880s, shows Mr. Chilman, the grocer, standing under a ham, and a rather smaller figure keeping guard over Mr. Holden's boots and shoes.

20 Hatch Mill in Mill Lane, now used for offices and storage. Parts of the building are 17th-century, as are the Dutch-inspired mill-workers' cottages on the left. The firm of J.C. Withers owned the mill from 1906 till 1965, and also had a corn and feed store in the High Street.

Old Watermill
Godalming

21 A drawing of the mill-wheel at Hatch Mill. The Ock stream was dammed into a millpond to ensure a steady flow of water. The wheel was replaced by a turbine in 1940 and the mill was able to operate for another ten years.

22 An impression drawn for an American architects' journal of how Westbrook Place may have appeared during James Oglethorpe's lifetime. It was built in 1671 and has since been almost totally reconstructed.

23 Admiral Sir John Balchin was born into a fairly humble Godalming family in 1670 and joined the Navy at the age of fourteen. In 1744 he commanded the *Victory* on a successful expedition to Portugal, but on the way home the ship and all her crew were lost in a storm. There is a memorial to the Admiral in Westminster Abbey.

24 (*right*) The upper High Street, *c*.1910. Before the setts were put in, this section was called Sand Street. The building in the centre started as an 18th-century town house, and in the 19th century it belonged to the Stedman family who ran a wine shop there. It became the post office in 1906 and remained such until 1994.

25 (*below*) Looking upstream at Catteshall lock in about 1903. This is the 16th and last lock between the Thames and Godalming Wharf, a distance of nearly 20 miles with a rise of 100 ft. The onlooker now would see narrow boats and cruisers moored along the bank, serviced at the boatyard behind the photographer. This part of the Navigation opened in 1764.

Godalming, Catteshall Lock

26 (*below*) Godalming Wharf was constructed primarily for the shipment of Wealden timber to the shipyards on the Thames. Gradually the process reversed and during this century horse-drawn barges were bringing imported timber up to yards like this one, Gridley and Spring's. The barge traffic lasted till 1925.

RIVER WEY
AND WHARF
GODALMING

27 (*right*) Possibly the earliest picture of Godalming parish church, dated 1771. It is a plate from *Twelve Views in Surry* [sic] *and Kent, drawn from Nature by J. Clevely junr.*. Art may have triumphed over accuracy.

28 (*below*) The shop fronts come and go but the history of the town remains visible in the upper storeys. The building on the right was a coaching inn—the *Great George*, while next but one along can be seen the elegant building which was once the *Little George*.

29 (*below*) Demolition under way at Busbridge Hall in 1906. The house dated mainly from 1775 and had had many owners including Emma Susan Ramsden who founded both the church and the school at Busbridge. A replacement Hall was built nearby.

30 The Town Bridge, built in 1782, marks the head of navigation on the River Wey. Until the A3 Guildford bypass was constructed, the bridge used to carry all the London—Portsmouth traffic. An earlier bridge was used only in conditions of flood: at other times coaches and wagons crossed by the ford. The photograph was taken in 1895.

31 Four horses pull a stage coach into Godalming while the reapers are busy on the Lammas land. In August, after the crops were harvested, the meadows would be opened to anyone who had grazing rights. The Little Fort, guarding Westbrook Place when it was the home of the Oglethorpe sisters, is prominent on the hillside in this engraving of 1799.

32 James Moon was landlord of the *King's Arms* in 1698 when Czar Peter the Great stayed there, but this advertising card must have been produced by a later Moon, since Bognor was not on the coaching map until Sir Richard Hotham started to develop it in 1788. Bognor Rocks themselves were a rather over-rated tourist attraction.

Direct Road from London to Portsmouth.

Harden, Griffin Kingston	12
Harden & Moon, Talbot Ripley	12
MOON, Kings Arms, Godalming	10
Billet, Anchor Liphook	12
Patrick, Dolphin Petersfield	8
Portsmouth	18
	72 Miles

Direct Road from London to Bognor Rocks.

MOON, Kings Arms Godalming	34
Steer, Half Moon Petworth	16
Bognor Rocks	18
	Miles 68

To Bognor by way of Chichester.

Kings Arms Godalming	34
Whitehorse Haslemere	9
Angel Eagle } Midhurst	8
Swan Dolphin } Chichester	11
Bognor Rocks	8
	Miles 70

GODALMING *December 15th 1803.*

BEING convinced of the impropriety of opening our Shops on the Morning of the Sabbath Day: WE the undersigned Tradesmen of the Town of GODALMING, take this method of reſpectfully informing our Cuſtomers, that our Shops will not be opened on that Day, after the end of the preſent year 1803.

ROBERT MOLINE, *Grocer.*

JOHN TASKER, *Draper.*

JAMES WEALE, *Ditto.*

JOHN COOKE, *Shop-keeper.*

JOHN WHITE, *Grocer.*

E. and R. STEDMAN, *Silverſmiths and Bookſellers.*

THOMAS COOKE, *Bookſeller, &c.*

JOHN PEACOCK, *Cabinet Maker.*

JOSEPH WESTBROOK, *Shop-keeper.*

WILLIAM PETO, *Ironmonger.*

JAMES COLBROOK, *Ditto.*

CHARLES SOAN, *Taylor and Salesman.*

Ruſſell, Printers, Guildford

33 This drawing, *c.*1800, shows an intrepid lady, carrying what looks like a water jug, walking between animals grazing on the town meadows. On the left is Church House and the two great plane trees, one of which now remains. To the right is the Parsonage House which, with its cottage and barn, was demolished in 1865.

34 Never on a Sunday. It has taken 192 years for the nation to overcome its sense of impropriety in this respect.

35 The late medieval Hundred House, later referred to as Market House, was the centre of town life. It covered the market and held a court room, lock-up, stocks, clock, water pump and bell.

Godalming.

Notice is hereby given, that a Meeting of the Inhabitants of this Town and Parish will be held in the TOWN HALL, on *Wednesday* the 27th. of *July*, inst. at eleven o'clock in the forenoon; to take into consideration the state of the present Market House, which has been represented to be ruinous and unsafe.

Thomas Haines,
WARDEN.

JULY 21. 1814.

Russells Printers, Guildford.

36 At the meeting the decision was taken to demolish the old building and put a slightly smaller one—the present Pepperpot—in its place, for which the sum of £783 7s. 2d. was raised by public subscription.

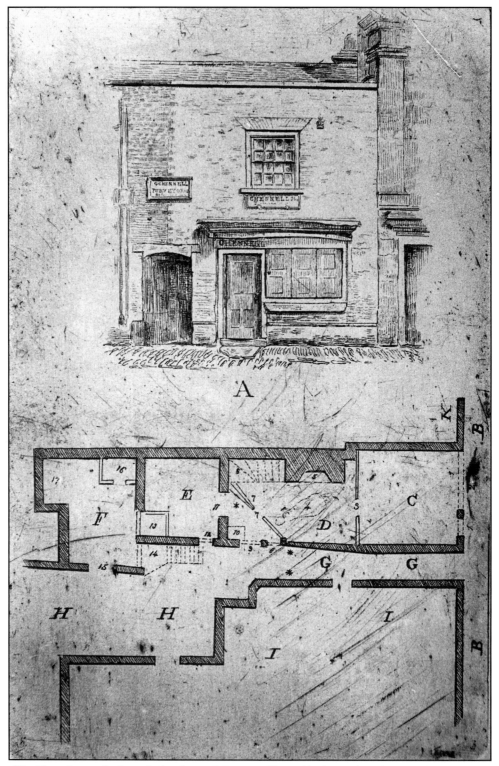

37 Elevation and plan of the shop of George Chennell, shoemaker, in Godalming High Street. He was murdered here along with Elizabeth Wilson his house—keeper, by his son, George Chennell junior, and his carter William Chalcraft on 10 November 1817. The outline of the housekeeper's body has been marked where it was found in room D. The two criminals were tried in Guildford and hanged on the Godalming Lammas land, the town's last public execution. Subsequently the beam of the gallows was thriftily placed as a supporting rafter in the church spire, where it is still doing duty.

GODALMING CHURCH. S.W.

Ground Plan.

38 A lithograph of 1824 showing the church of St Peter and St Paul from the south west. The nave was extended westwards in 1840 and the porch replaced by the present one in 1911. The yew tree is still there. The 14th-century bell cote at the base of the spire was removed in 1850 but has now been restored.

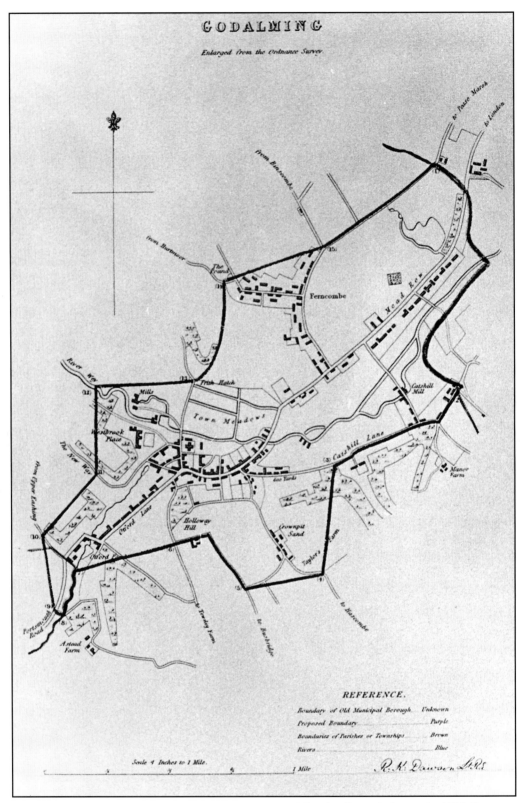

39 A map showing the Borough boundary proposed by the Commissioners in 1835. It was not implemented and there was no official boundary drawn until 1892. The Borough was enlarged in 1929 and 1933 to bring in new residential areas, and roadside cast-iron boundary posts bearing these dates can be seen in various places.

40 The church of St John the Evangelist, Farncombe, pictured here at about the turn of the century, was built to a design by Sir George Gilbert Scott on land presented by James More Molyneux of Loseley, who laid the foundation stone in 1846. The ecclesiastical parish of Farncombe was set up in 1849.

41 A few railway trucks were scattered about the sidings at Godalming old station in 1936. This was the 1849 terminus of the L.S.W.R. which handled passenger traffic till 1897 and continued as a goods depot until 1969.

42 The old *Railway Hotel*, opened in 1849 to welcome passengers arriving at the terminus, was rebuilt after a fire in the 1930s and is now called the *Wey Inn*. Beyond it was the *Fountain*.

43 The date, 1854, makes this one of the earliest photographs of any Surrey street. The photographer was H.C. Malden, a schoolmaster who retired to Godalming and became a town councillor and a J.P. It is good to find that the High Street is still instantly recognisable except that the white house has been exchanged for the old Waitrose building.

44 Godalming station opened in January 1859, and is pictured here, *c.*1900. There was a level crossing just beyond it at the top of Mill Lane, removed in 1937. The whole building was recently renovated in a joint operation by British Rail and Friary Meux, brewers, whose offices were just across the road.

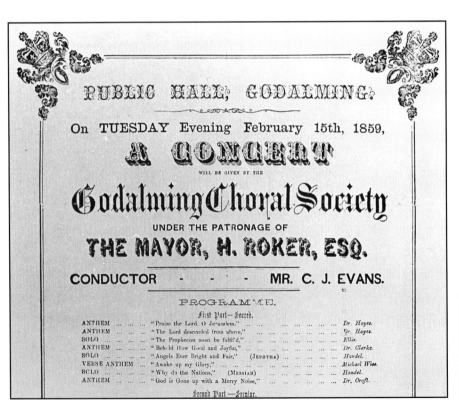

45 Posters advertising concerts by the Godalming Choral Society still appear on the town's notice boards, though there have been gaps in its existence. There is a strong tradition of music-making in the town, encouraged by the contribution of Charterhouse.

46   The short stretch of railway line between Farncombe and Godalming stations was an expensive undertaking, calling for a cutting, an embankment, three brick arch bridges and two girder bridges, the one over Borough Road seen here. Nightingale Road had to be taken over the line and the Manor Road footbridge was added later.

47   The old cemetery in Nightingale Road with its chapel of rest. It contains the graves of Philip Heseltine, better known as the composer Peter Warlock, Arthur Clutton-Brock the poet and critic who once lived in the Red House, and Percy Woods, Godalming's own historian. The graveyard at the parish church was closed in 1857.

48 (*right*) Godalming in the 1860s. The station had not long been built; beyond it the railway line continued as single track to Havant. Borough Road had not appeared, though the bridge was ready for it, and grazing land came down to the southern edge of the town. The parish church was covered in the stucco of the 1840 remodelling, which was removed in 1879.

49 (*below*) The cart track to Deanery Farm seen from the new railway bridge in about 1860. The track became Borough Road and the farmhouse is now no. 46 Charterhouse Road. The barn was restored by Hugh Thackeray Turner and given to the St Peter and St Paul scouts, who still use it.

50 (*below*) Here the track from Deanery Farm and Frith Hill reaches the town. Farm wagons forded the river below Boarden Bridge which is still in use though now overshadowed by the Borough Road bridge built in 1870. This photograph was taken from the new railway embankment.

CRICKET.

A Grand Match

WILL BE PLAYED AT

BROADWATER, GODALMING,

On MONDAY, SEPTEMBER 7th, 1863, and two following Days.

BETWEEN THE

UNITED ALL ENGLAND ELEVEN.

AND SIXTEEN OF

GODALMING AND DISTRICT.

GODALMING, & DISTRICT.	UNITED ALL ENGLAND.
COLONEL F. MARSHALL	W. CAFFYN
CAPTAIN H. MARSHALL	W. MORTLOCK
MAJOR WOLFE	R. CARPENTER
CAPTAIN INGE	T. LOCKYER
CAPTAIN N. W. WALLACE	T. HEARNE
E. DOWSON, Esq.	G. ATKINSON
T. C. GOODRICH, Esq.	T. SEWELL
E. M. GRACE, Esq.	C. ELLIS
J. BURNETT, Esq.	G. BENNETT
C. CALVERT, Esq.	J. LILLYWHITE
E. BARRETT, Esq.	J. WISDEN
JULIUS CAESAR	J. GRUNDY
H. H. STEPHENSON	
O GRIFFITH	
T. HUMPHREY	
H. JUPP	

Refreshments & Good Accommodation provided on the Ground.

DINNER PUNCTUALLY AT HALF-PAST TWO.

Admission Sixpence each. Gentlemen on Horse-back, 1s. One Horse Chaise including Driver, 1s. 6d. Two Horse ditto including Driver, 2s. 6d.

[STEDMAN, PRINTER, GODALMING.]

51 Ancient and modern. Another picture of the wooden Boarden Bridge which for centuries carried the path to Frith Hill over the river. It still does so while traffic uses the brick Borough Road bridge, built to connect with Charterhouse. Its unnecessary height has earned it the nickname 'Lunatic Bridge'.

52 The Godalming 16 won this match by 44 runs. Broadwater, long since demolished, was the home of a branch of the Marshall family. Julius Caesar (1830-1878), Godalming's greatest cricketer, also played for Surrey and England, and finished his career as cricket coach at Charterhouse.

53 A late 19th-century etching of *The New Charterhouse*. P.C. Hardwick's Bargate-stone building was completed in 1872 in time to receive Dr. Haig-Brown and his 153 boys. Three boarding houses were included in the original building; others appeared along Frith Hill and down Charterhouse Road as the number of boys increased.

54 The first of a row of buildings on the eastern side of Bridge Road was built as the British School in 1813 and remodelled in 1872. In Victorian times it was the fierce rival of the Bell School in Moss Lane. It subsequently became a County Primary school, then a Roman Catholic junior school, and is now part of the Adult Education complex.

55 (*above*) At the eastern end of Frith Hill this outcrop of Lower Greensand can still be seen, now covered by ivy which seems to deter the sandmartins which once nested there. On the other side of the hill was a Bargate stone quarry which supplied much of the building material for houses in the area at the end of the 19th century.

56 (*above*) The Catteshall water turbine awaiting reassembly. It was installed in Spicer's paper mill in 1869, having been built in Belfast to a French design. The mill subsequently became Blackburn's foundry and the turbine was used to drive a dynamo until 1970. It was scheduled as an ancient monument and removed to its present site in 1981.

57 (*left*) The Godalming Brass Band, predecessor of the present Town Band, was founded by William Woodnutt in 1844 and is pictured here some 20 years later at the bottom of Brighton Road in front of houses now demolished for the relief road. The dog seems to have them well under control.

58 Salgasson Mill, part of the Westbrook mills complex, was built on the site of a medieval fulling mill. It was a corn mill until 1875, about the date of this picture, and then was converted to use for leather dressing by the Pullman brothers. It was just below here that electricity was generated for the world's first public supply.

59 A famous picture published in *The Graphic* in November 1881. Using current generated by water power at R. & J. Pullman's mill, the upper part of the town was lit by three lamps, and Godalming had achieved world fame.

60 The Godalming Gas & Coke Co. Ltd. supplied the town's lighting from 1836 till the coming of electricity in 1881, then again from 1884 till 1897. Gas for heating continued to be produced until nationalisation. The present police station was built on the derelict site in 1968.

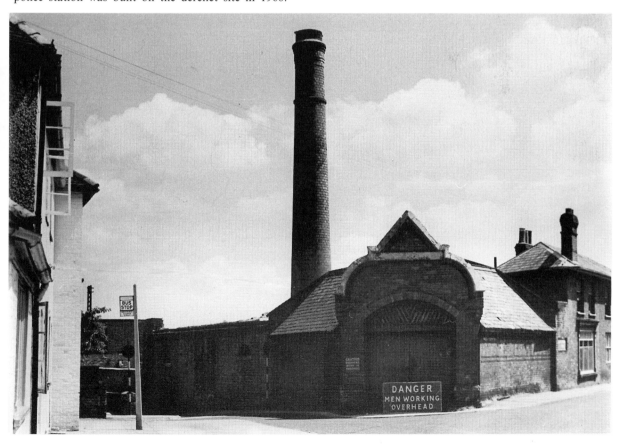

61 Victoria Road is a curving cul-de-sac built on the site of cowsheds and a slaughterhouse in 1887. It was in a world of its own beyond the gas works. On this side of the gas holders ran the road known as The Wharf, now upgraded to carry all the A3100 traffic.

62 Holloway Hill in the late 19th century at the point where approaching travellers got their first glimpse of the town, now just below St Hilary's School. It was a main track into and out of Godalming since Saxon times. There were Bargate stone quarries at the top and the bottom of the hill.

63 Looking along Borough Road in the 1890s, 20 years after the Borough Council decided to construct it. Houses have begun to appear along the crest of Frith Hill, and at the cross-roads the *Charterhouse Arms* is already serving the needs of the new community.

64 Town End Street under construction in the late 19th century, looking towards the junction with Brighton Road. Bargate stone broken to two-and-a-quarter-inch gauge was still being used as the basic road-building material, but this was found to be too soft as motor traffic increased, and harder stone had to be imported from the Midlands or Cornwall.

65 A carefully posed picture showing Town End Street completed, this time looking towards the town. Town End was previously the name of a large field where fairs and circuses were sometimes held.

66 The staff at Godalming old station, *c.*1885. Now a housing development called Old Station Way, this was the terminus of the London and South Western Railway from 1849-59.

67 This late 19th-century picture shows that Godalming was indeed a working town with factory chimneys rivalling the church spire. The millpond on the Ock provided power for Hatch Mill. On the left is Allen, Solly & Co.'s former hosiery factory. The firm moved to Nottingham in 1888 and bequeathed a knitting machine to Godalming Museum.

68 High Street in 1895, paved with granite setts. The balcony above the butcher's shop marks the end of a row of buildings put up by the Skinners' Company in 1836. Beyond is the Capital and Counties Bank (now Lloyds). A lady remembers her great uncle recounting how he used to hold customers' horses outside the bank for a penny.

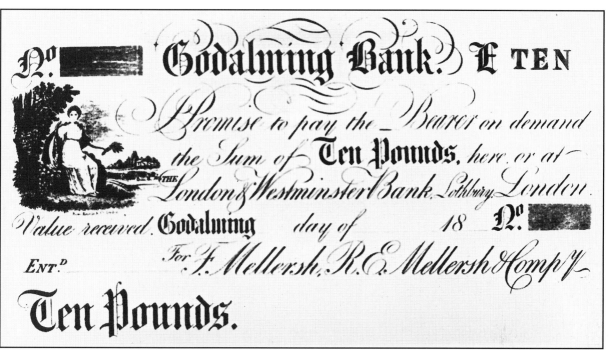

69 The brothers Robert and Frederick Mellersh ran the Godalming Bank, founded by their father in 1808, from about 1840 to 1893 when it was bought by the Capital and Counties, which merged with Lloyds Bank in 1918. Lloyds still operates in the same High Street premises.

70 In 1892 Westbrook Place, former home of the Oglethorpe family, was bought by the Countess of Meath and turned into a home for epileptic women. In August of that year it was officially opened by Queen Victoria's daughter, the Duchess of Albany—another excuse for Godalming to get out the decorations.

71 Westbrook Place seen soon after its reopening as the Meath Home in 1892. Nathaniel Godbold, commemorated in the parish church as 'inventor and proprietor of that excellent medicine the vegetable balsam for the cure of consumptions and asthmas', bought the house after James Oglethorpe's death in 1785 and had it practically rebuilt. Further alterations were made in the 19th century.

72 This building in Bridge Road, now part of the Waverley Adult Education complex, was put up in 1896 as a technical institute. Fee-paying students were given further education in business and craft skills. It is a dominating building seen across the Lammas land and nowadays might have trouble getting planning permission.

73 The little shop next to the old *White Hart* is known as Griggs, a name which can be traced back to late medieval times. At the time of this photograph, *c.*1895, it was being run as a greengrocery by the Misses Luxford.

74 In the 1890s the western end of Godalming was dominated by Rea Sons and Fisher's tannery in Mill Lane. This view shows Holloway Hill running down to its junction with the upper High Street. On its right can be seen the old buildings and trees of Rock Place on the line of the future Flambard Way.

General View of Godalming No.1.

75 Washing day in Victoria Road at the eastern end of the town. Prominent features are the gas works, the spire of the Congregational church and, in front of it, the old cart shed of the Godalming Navigation. Charterhouse shows up on the skyline.

76 Mill Lane, *c*.1900. The little group are standing on the bridge over the Ock in front of Hatch Mill. The first Saxon settlement was probably on the slope beyond them. Behind the cottages to the right is the 18th-century Friends' Meeting House in the area known as The Mint.

General View of Godalming No. 3.

77 (*above*) When Frith Hill was first developed in the 1870s people were able to build large houses to live in, such as the one in this photograph. Now these have nearly all been demolished or divided into flats. In the foreground are Dean Lodge and Deanery Farmhouse with its outbuildings.

78 There seems to have been no problem about closing the High Street for Queen Victoria's Diamond Jubilee celebrations in 1897. Feasting took place behind this splendid façade fixed on a marquee which stretched from the *Angel* hotel to Pound Lane.

79 Looking towards the Pepperpot in 1897 with the town bedecked for the Diamond Jubilee. The old *White Hart* is nearly hidden behind the Stars and Stripes. One admires the discipline imposed by the photographer: even the police sergeant has eyes for no one else.

80 A late Victorian view of the Brighton Road. At that time there were several businesses in this area: two pubs, a cobbler, a barber, a vet and a sweetshop. Behind the photographer is Crownpits Green, the town's first public open space, bought by the Council for £325 in 1910.

81 All the late 19th-century building along Peperharow Road was on the north side. The alluvial land on the left was known as Salgassons. At the time of this picture the main entrance to Charterhouse was by what is now the back drive off Peperharow Road.

82 The road to Hambledon, *c.*1904, once the main route from Godalming to Petworth. This is a typical Surrey hollow way, worn down into the soft Greensand by water, feet, hooves and wheels.

83 An unchanging view across the Lammas land. There are various owners of the land, which was registered under the Commons Registration Act of 1965, but nobody was able to show that they had Commoner's rights. The stream across the middle is known as Hell Ditch.

84 A delightful picture taken at the beginning of this century. The old frontage of the *White Hart* on the right and the *Angel* opposite, as well as the sheep themselves, are all reminders of local history. Perhaps it is tactless to mention that there were several slaughter-houses in the town.

85 The Red House on Frith Hill is the only major Lutyens building within the town boundary. It was built in 1899 for Mr. Evans, a Charterhouse master who was crippled and required a special staircase with shallow steps. Some of the features appear in Castle Drogo, built on a similar hilltop site in Devon.

86 Dr. and Mrs. Hedley Burrows. He was one of 53 vicars of Godalming whose names are recorded in the parish church, holding office from 1888 to 1904. He became Suffragan Bishop of Lewes and subsequently Bishop of Sheffield, a post he held till 1939.

87 Lord Baden-Powell, Chief Scout and hero of the relief of Mafeking, had been one of the Charterhouse boys who moved to Godalming in 1872. Here, in 1901, he is seen leaving Godalming vicarage to lay the foundation stone of the school's Boer War memorial.

88 This view of Charterhouse Road from the bridge was unchanged for nearly 100 years. On the left was the Bodeites kitchen garden, off to the right were Lockites and Weekites. On the skyline is the Frith Hill water tower, built in 1880. Now there are houses on the left, flats on the right, and the water tower is decommissioned though listed.

89 The Godalming fire brigade, with spectators, seen in 1904 with their new horse-drawn steam pump. Later that year they moved from the Wharf to a new fire station in Queen Street.

90 The site of Mr. Enticknap's haulage and blacksmith's business is unrecognisable today. It was in Rock Place, just about on the line of Flambard Way coming to the Holloway Hill traffic lights. The photograph dates from about 1900.

91 Mr. Joe Enticknap, wearing a straw hat and a watch chain which is now in the possession of his grandson, seen with members of his quoits team in 1903. Matches were sometimes played in pub gardens, such as that at the *Tanners' Arms* in Meadrow.

92 Looking across the Lammas land from the Town Bridge in about 1900. The river had not been embanked, while Chalk Road had only recently been constructed. The houses at the *Charterhouse Arms* corner can be seen in the distance beyond the railway.

93 The eastern end of the High Street in about 1903, showing the *Sun* inn closing the view and, nearer the camera, the *King's Arms* and the *Woolpack*. All three are still in business. On the left is the shop of George West in the premises where he worked as a photographer from 1882 to 1920.

94 The most altered part of the High Street, seen about 90 years ago. The house with the little garden belonged to Dr. Parsons, whose daughter used to ride about the town with her pack of Dalmatians. The building containing Tanner's shop became the library. In the 1960s both were swept away to be replaced by Waitrose.

95 The *Squirrel Inn* at Hurtmore early in the 20th century. Thirty years later the A3 Guildford and Godalming bypass came past just behind the pub, which entered a new period of prosperity. Two of Godalming's most productive Bargate stone quarries were nearby.

96 The Oak Bark Tannery, off Mill Lane, had a major fire in 1905 and never really recovered, though the leather trade lingered on in Godalming till 1957, represented by Messrs C.M. Gay who processed rabbit skins for the hat trade. Arden House, formerly Hatch House, is seen on the right during its days as the *Railway Hotel*.

97 Craddock's, the printers, published a series of invaluable Godalming directories from 1868 to 1913. They listed all the businesses and householders in the town, besides printing poems, jokes and so forth. The firm moved to larger premises before the Second World War.

98   A page of advertisements in Craddock's Godalming directory of 1913.

99 An Edwardian idyll. Ever since pleasure boating became popular, the river Wey with its controlled current and shady banks has been a great asset to Godalming people looking for a few hours' relaxation.

100 This Edwardian picture shows the spire of the Congregational church in the distance and the Methodist church of 1903 on the left. The spire was removed as a safety measure and the building is now a sale room. In 1977 the congregation of what had become the United Reformed Church moved across the river and joined the Methodists to become the Godalming United Church.

101 A splendidly inappropriate picture to convey Christmas greetings, this card was posted on 21 December 1905. It shows Farncombe station which had been opened eight years before, on the same day that the old Godalming terminus behind the *Railway Hotel* closed to passenger traffic.

102 No. 572, here looking very spick and span, was one of a class of tank engines built for the London, Brighton and South Coast Railway early in the 20th century. They were named after Surrey stations even though some, like this one, were served by a rival line. They were robust machines and some lasted into the 1950s.

103 (*right*) Looking along Meadrow early in this century, with the *Fountain* inn sign on the left, we see the fine line-up of Mr. Nash's vehicles for hire—two horseless carriages and about a dozen of the more traditional sort. He must have been disappointed when the old station nearby was closed to passenger traffic in 1897.

104 (*below*) Farncombe Street early in the 20th century was a mixture of shops, many of them branches of ones in Godalming, and private houses with gardens. The *Duke of Wellington* had opened for business, up on the right, and until 1903 there was a Methodist chapel lower down. The old manor pound and 17th- and 18th-century cottages were further up the hill.

105 (*below*) Lower Farncombe Street, *c*.1910. The railway signal box can be seen at the top. On the right where the Station Garage now stands was Farncombe House, at that time the home of Dr. Boyd, a well-known Godalming figure. Beyond the *Royal Oak* was a branch of Gammons the drapers, run by the parents of Jack Phillips of *Titanic* fame.

106 This little group are standing at the top of Holloway Hill near to where Tuesley Lane and Busbridge Lane diverge. In 1910 the predecessor of St Hilary's School was started in the third house, just out of sight to the left.

107 In 1936, long after this postcard was sent, St Hilary's School moved down the hill to the larger premises of Kilcott, whose entrance can be seen on the left. The top of Holloway Hill is some 200 feet higher than the town centre and in most photographs of it there is a seated figure getting its breath back.

108 Looking down the Brighton Road towards the town in 1908. It was not unusual to find pubs next door to each other, as here the *Three Crowns* and the *Queen's Head*, each catering for its own clientèle, but it was less common that they should belong to the same brewery, in this case Friary. Both have gone since the last war.

109 Croft Road was constructed in late Victorian times. It took its name from *The Croft*, a private house fronting onto the High Street. An earlier sale of the property described it as having a garden and hop ground well planted with fruit trees. In their place is St Edmund's Roman Catholic church built in 1906.

110 The straight lines of Queen Street show it to be a comparative newcomer. It was constructed in 1887 and named Jubilee Street. It joined Croft Road to the High Street but has now been bisected by Flambard Way so that only pedestrians can traverse the full length.

111 Queen Street, *c.*1910. The fire station is on the left; when the hooter sounded people used to gather outside the *King's Arms* at the end of the street to see how long it took the engine to appear with its bell clanging. Beyond the cart also on the left is Victoria Motor Works where a rather unsuccessful motor car used to be assembled.

112 Since 1911 there has been a gap in the row of cottages in Ockford Road because in that year the *Anchor* inn was demolished and rebuilt further back to allow for a service and parking area.

113 St John's Street in Farncombe has changed little in appearance since the early years of the 20th century, apart from the coming of sodium lights. It is remarkable how the appearance of a camera seemed to bring all life to a standstill.

114 This postcard showing Peperharow Road was posted at 2.30 p.m. on 31 December 1907, the sender confident that her New Year greetings would be received next day. The tower on the skyline was filled with water pumped up from low-lying ground to the right of the picture.

115 This view of Bridge Street, *c*.1910, shows the newly built municipal buildings on the right and, on the left, a fine mixture of businesses including a pub, the *West Surrey House*. All these nearer shops would soon be replaced by the Godalming and District Co-op.

116 September 1968. A reminder that at one time Bridge Street used to be called Water Lane. There are many locks and sluices between Godalming and the Thames, calling for a complicated system for controlling the water flow in times of flood. On this occasion it seemed to work to Godalming's disadvantage.

117 By 1908 Charterhouse Road had taken shape, climbing up under the bridge to Markway and on by Hurtmore. The line of Frith Hill Road, then known as Hindhead Road, can be followed on the right past Hodgsonites, Bodeites and the Red House. Aldous Huxley, whose father taught at Charterhouse, was born in a house behind these on Farncombe Hill.

118   A tarring machine developed by Mr. F.G. Barnes, founder of a motor engineering business in Godalming. It was pulled by a steam roller, with the steam used to heat the tar. Here it is being demonstrated on the Portsmouth Road near Milford in 1910. The well-dressed spectators are mostly local government officers, and several machines were ordered including one for Godalming.

119   The owner of Thorn's Dining Rooms in Church Street standing in the doorway with his family in 1907. Hot meals were served all day every day and the Rooms became affiliated to the Cyclists' Touring Club. Young Dicky (on the right) took over the business after the Great War and ran it until his retirement in 1973.

120 Charles Burgess was Mayor six times between 1885 and 1927. His Borough Stores, with meat and grocery departments, occupied the present Boots site in the High Street until the 1960s. This fine Christmas display, which is making the dog look rather wistful, must have relied on the weather staying cold.

121 An advertising card for Ockford Mill which was taken on by George Cole in 1907. It has now been converted to offices. This is one of four mills that were powered by the Ock stream, aided by a large millpond which now serves as a backdrop to the *Inn on the Lake*.

122 Busbridge Hall, on the outskirts of Godalming, was built in 1906 to replace the 18th-century Hall which stood down by the lake, one of a chain of four in the landscaped park which has been enclosed since the 17th century. The house is now a nursing home.

123 Looking up Pound Lane towards the forge which later added a riding school to its activities and lasted until the 1950s. The site of the original manorial pound was sold in 1792 and the enclosure was moved once or twice more before settling in its present position in Brighton Road.

124 Llanaway Cottages, Meadrow, were built in 1875 through the generosity of the Hallam sisters. The cottages were endowed as accommodation for elderly people and are still administered as a charity.

125 Meadrow School was built in 1907 on land which was formerly a small dairy farm belonging to Llanaway House, sold after Miss Hallam died. The school started as an offshoot of the council school in Bridge Road and later became a County Secondary school, the predecessor of Broadwater.

126 Designed in 1906 by the Borough Surveyor, J.H. Norris, the municipal buildings included a council chamber and offices grouped round a private dwelling called the Stone House, and incorporated an existing public hall, seen on the right. The buildings now link onto the Waverley Borough Council offices at the back.

127 In 1910 there were plenty of craft for hire at the Catteshall landing stage. At that time barges were still plying up the river to Godalming Wharf. The towpath can be seen on the left heading down towards Guildford.

128　1910. Well-drilled schoolchildren have formed fours to march to the Old Town Hall to hear the Mayor read
the proclamation of the accession of King George V in 1910—a serious occasion, with rejoicing postponed till the
coronation. On the right is the private front garden of the house called The Croft.

129 The cloister was built in 1913 to a design by Hugh Thackeray Turner in memory of Jack Phillips, chief telegraphist on the *Titanic* which sank in 1912. He was born and brought up in Farncombe and attended Godalming Grammar School. The fountain was provided by the Postal Telegraph Clerks Association. Gertrude Jekyll designed the surrounding garden.

130 A picture taken from the spire of the parish church showing the Phillips Memorial Cloister with one side and the central pond removed to deter vandalism. The old Rectory Manor pound was moved to make way for the path and was rebuilt round the lime tree.

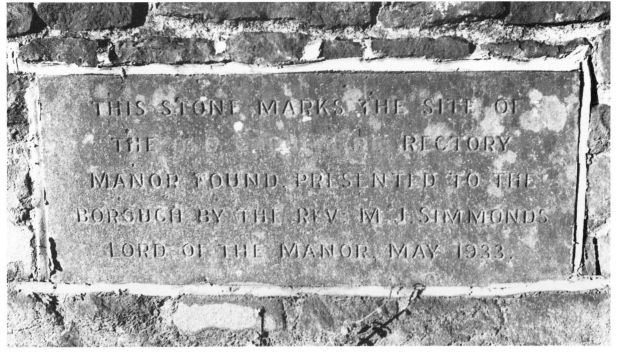

131 A stone let into the wall of the Rectory Manor pound records its donation to the town by the Rev. Mark Simmonds in 1933. He lived in Church House and was a great benefactor to the townspeople.

132 Since early Victorian times the main town centre roads had been surfaced with granite setts, ordered by the Commissioners for watching, lighting and paving. This picture of 1913 shows the setts being replaced with tarred wooden blocks. Two men hold axes for making final adjustments to the blocks.

133 The Catteshall Coffee Tavern was an imposing building on the corner of Meadrow and Catteshall Road. Before the Great War there was a strong temperance movement in the town, and for its adherents this coffee tavern provided a welcome alternative to the numerous inns.

134 This card was posted just before the outbreak of war in 1914. Even then, as now, a car parked in the narrow High Street could cause a traffic jam. Burgess' grocery store was on the right beyond Moss Lane, and opposite can be seen Mather, the chemist, and Jones, ironmonger's.

135 Lord Kitchener was appointed War Minister as soon as war was declared in 1914, and the famous 'Your Country needs You' poster was issued on 7 August. The call for volunteers to enlist was so effective that it was not necessary to introduce conscription until March 1916.

Special Recruiting Committee.

Borough Hall, Godalming,
August 20th, 1914.

Sir,

With reference to Lord Kitchener's Appeal for Recruits, which doubtless you have seen in the public press, would you be so kind as to inform this Committee, which, to prevent overlapping, is acting on behalf

of {
The Borough Council,
The County Territorial Association,
The National Service League,
The Local Recruiting Committee,

whether you are disposed to offer facilities to those in your employ between the ages of 19 and 30 to join :—

1. Lord Kitchener's New Army for the period of the War, or
2. The Territorial Force (now embodied),

and to use your great influence with them to encourage them to offer their services for the above branches of His Majesty's Forces.

Any information with which you are good enough to furnish this Committee will be treated as confidential.

Any further particulars as to eligibility for service to the country of any nature will be gladly furnished by this Committee.

Yours very faithfully,

Hon. Sec.,
Special Recruiting Committee.

To ....

....

....

136 The ladies of Godalming and Guildford playing cricket on Holloway Hill recreation ground in 1916 in aid of the prisoners of war fund. The ground, which belonged to the Godalming Recreation Club Co. Ltd., was dug up to grow vegetables during the war but the cricket square was left intact.

137 A country fit for heroes. One hundred and five names appear on the 1914-18 war memorial. Those who returned were welcomed to a dinner held in the Victoria Hall, Queen Street, in 1919. The premises then returned to the job of repairing motor cars while a church hall was built on the other side of the street to cater for the social life.

Godalming's Dinner to Ex Service men

138 Mr. Burgess, fifth from the left in the group of competitors all stripped to the waistcoat, was in his penultimate period as Mayor in 1919. After his final term of office he was elected a Freeman of the Borough, a very rare honour. The Peace Sports were held at the Catteshall sports ground.

139 This peaceful view of Church Street was sent to British Columbia on 4 January 1919. Headed Witley Camp it says ' ... today I was put on draft for Canada. Three cheers! Expect to leave here for a port of embarkation Feb. 10th. Regards to all Leo xxx.'

140 Busbridge church soon after acquiring its Lutyens war memorial in 1922. The church, of Bargate stone, was designed by George Gilbert Scott and consecrated in 1867. It was paid for by Mrs. Ramsden who was also instrumental in starting the village school across the road. The churchyard contains the tombs of Gertrude Jekyll and other members of her family.

141 Gertrude Jekyll aged about 40, *c.*1880, when she was best known as an artist and writer. It was only later, as failing eyesight forced her to give up close work, that she let her interest in gardening become a full-time occupation. She lived in Munstead, on the outskirts of Godalming, and planned many gardens to complement houses designed by her friend Edwin Lutyens.

142 Charterhouse chapel was built in the 1920s as a memorial of Old Carthusians who died in the Great War. It was designed by Sir Giles Gilbert Scott. There are nearly 700 names on a list which starkly brings home the tragedy of war.

Godalming, Market House.

143   Plenty of room on top! Soon after the Great War, during which it may have done military service, a bone-shaking omnibus of the Aldershot and District Traction Co. Ltd. waits at the Pepperbox for anyone wanting to go to Guildford. On the left is the *Skinners' Arms*, one of at least 15 town-centre pubs to have closed within living memory.

144   Charterhouse bridge is still in place but Hindhead Road, to the left, was considered to be misleadingly named and became Frith Hill Road in 1921. It is now blocked off below the Charterhouse entrance.

145 A day's outing in 1920 would go to Southsea or Bognor; a shorter trip might take a picnic to Frensham
Ponds. One imagines there must have been much clutching at hats as the charabanc gathered speed.

146 Quarrymen of the 1920s preparing to extract a lump of Bargate stone, known as a dogger, from its bed of Greensand, probably in Hurtmore quarry. They would balance themselves with their poles, then jump up and down on the plank until the stone behind them was levered loose.

147 A Bargate stone quarry at Hurtmore, which was one of four operating until 1939. By that time much of the stone was broken up and used for road making, and there was a steady demand from landscape gardeners. The mind recoils from the thought of pushing barrows full of stone along those planks.

148 Godalming station in the 1920s. In this scene the two gentlemen walking on the down platform are dressed for a day at the seaside, perhaps influenced by the Southsea poster outside the cloakroom.

149 A smart equipage crosses the Town Bridge. There seems plenty of room, but in 1926 an elderly citizen was crushed to death against the parapet by a timber wagon and the bridge was subsequently widened to take a footway on each side.

150 Cooper's shop, shown in the early 1920s, was the predecessor of Field Bros. and is now a baker's. It is much larger inside than the front suggests. The carrier's well-groomed horse had obviously learned to be patient.

151 The junction of Peperharow Road and Charterhouse Road, photographed in the early 1920s with the usual dog. Deanery Farmhouse and its barn stand back from the road beyond the terrace of houses. On the left is Dean Lodge, now demolished, at that time the home of Dr. Boyd and his family.

152 Carnival House in Catteshall Road was the first prize in a lottery during the 1924 carnival week. Tickets cost half-a-crown in aid of the Royal Surrey County Hospital Extension Fund. The winner was Mrs. Mackey whose family ran the forge and riding school in Pound Lane. The house was valued at £400.

153 The 1924 carnival week has stayed alive in the town's memory, perhaps because so many photographs of it were taken. The Carnival Queen was the daughter of Mr. Spring, the Mayor. Looking at this picture one must banish irreverent thoughts of seven maids with seven mops.

154 The Pears Soap float pauses for adjustment during the carnival procession. One hopes that the goat and its companion did not have to walk the full distance from Farncombe all the way through Godalming High Street and back.

155 The choir of St John's Church, Farncombe, photographed in 1930 with the rector, the Rev. Charles Knight. Some 30 years earlier the front row would have included Jack Phillips, who lived nearby. (*See* illustration 129.)

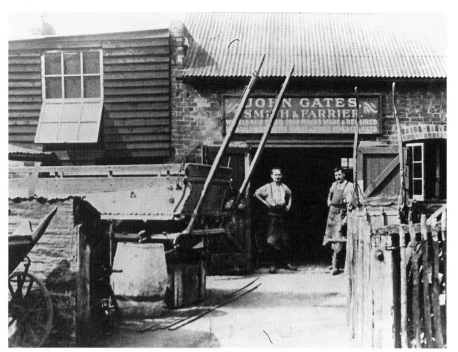

156 In the 1930s the Farncombe forge was in North Street behind the *Duke of Wellington*. Jack Gates, the blacksmith, was Captain of the Godalming fire brigade which had its station in Queen Street, so the sound of the alarm must have called for some fast pedalling.

157 Decorations for the Silver Jubilee in 1935 were restrained by Godalming standards. A quiet picture: no people, no traffic, no litter and, judging by the drawn blinds, no business expected at Feltham's shop—a family business which traded until 1964 as outfitters, furnishers, haberdashers and funeral directors.

158 The Regal cinema opened in 1935 and is now a bingo hall. It was preceded by Rudger's picture palace in Station Road which showed silent films to violin and piano accompaniment, and by the King George's cinema on Meadrow where there is now a supermarket. The design of the Regal had been approved, we are told, by Sir Edwin Lutyens.

REGAL
GODALMING

TELEPHONE No. 933.

Three Separate Performances Daily—at 2.30 p.m., 5.50 p.m. and 8.30 p.m.
Prices of Admission—Balcony 2/- and 1/6.   Stalls 1/6, 1/-, 9d. and 6d.

GRAND OPENING CEREMONY

Friday, 2nd August, at 8.15 p.m.

Doors open at 7.30 p.m.

by

HIS WORSHIP THE MAYOR OF GODALMING
Alderman W. F. Paine, J.P.

BAND and TRUMPETERS OF H.M. GRENADIER GUARDS

By kind permission of COL. G. E. C. RASCH, D.S.O.
Under the direction of MAJOR GEORGE MILLER, M.B.E.

LESLIE HOWARD and MERLE OBERON

in

"THE SCARLET PIMPERNEL."

The entire Proceeds from this performance will be given to the Royal Surrey County Hospital

159 The townsfolk gather at the Old Town Hall in 1936. Edward VIII was proclaimed King five days after the death of his father, George V. A sense of solemnity is strong in this photograph. Hats and robes (and the Town Clerk's wig) have been retained by the present Town Council as a reminder of continuity with the past.

160 An aerial photograph of the town in 1936 with the Pepperpot lower right and St Edmund's Church at the top. The 1991 relief road, Flambard Way, now runs through the centre of this picture, having caused the demolition of the Masonic Hall, Pitcher's factory and Stovold's dairy in Rock Place.

161 A jackdaw's view of the Burys from the church tower in 1936. In the picture are allotments, the bowling green, the Congregational school-house, buildings in Bridge Road and, far right, the chimney of Godalming laundry. The library, the Burys road, the riverside walk and Crown Court car park were not yet part of the scene.

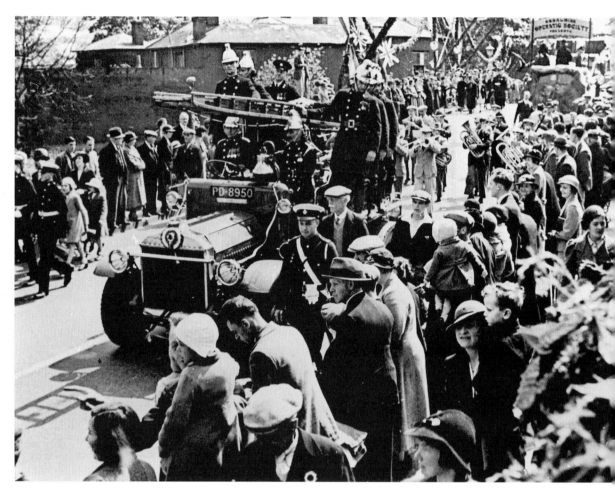

162 The ladies' hats show that we are approaching modern times. It is 1937 and the parade is to celebrate the coronation of King George VI. The Godalming fire brigade on their red Dennis engine lead the band past Bridge House. Further back is the float of the Godalming Operatic Society who performed their first Gilbert and Sullivan opera in 1925.

163 Coronation, 1937. Their Majesties' portraits adorn the Old Town Hall while the Mayor and Town Clerk pass by on their chargers, ahead of Queen Elizabeth I. Presumably the cheering throng was waiting further down the street.

164 The Mayor, P.C. Fletcher, who was a master at Charterhouse, and town councillors after attending a service at the school chapel on Coronation Sunday, 9 May 1937. Seated next to the Mayor is the Headmaster, Robert Birley.

165 Stovold's milk bar in Godalming High Street in 1938. The first milk bar opened in London in 1935 and the idea quickly gained approval, both for its contribution to a healthy diet and also as an agreeable meeting place.

166 This view of the High Street in the late 1930s shows its slightly sinuous line, indicative of an ancient street which has evolved rather than been designed. At that time cars parked on alternate sides of the road on odd and even dates.

167 Before the last war A.A. and R.A.C. scouts, with their sidecar motor bicycles, were much more than breakdown mechanics. They found many ways to help motorists, as this one was doing. They endeared themselves to Godalming members by not saluting if there was a police trap in the High Street.

The Pepper Box, Godalming.

copyright
GDG. 20.

168 Air Raid Precautions, 1939. The wardens of Post C5 based at the Coffee Tavern in Meadrow. More than 200 bombs fell on Godalming during the war, including ten on Charterhouse where a searchlight attracted the raiders' attention. No civilians were killed.

169 The Local Defence Volunteers were formed in May 1940 when invasion seemed imminent; they became known as the Home Guard in July. Any man between 17 and 65 who had not been called up could join. This group consisted of Southern Railway employees.

170 Past mayors look down on a meeting of Godalming Borough Council during the Second World War. Aldermen and councillors sit round in a hollow square with officers and press in the centre. The council chamber was first used in 1906 and was enlarged in 1979 to accommodate the 52 councillors of Waverley who came from Farnham, Haslemere, Cranleigh, Godalming and the villages between.

171 Post-war changes. Crown Court was once inhabited by weavers and frame-work knitters. In 1956 the north and south sides were knocked down to make an exit from the car park to the High Street, and this archway was built using the old materials.

172 Aldermen, in fur-trimmed robes, and councillors stand outside the Borough Hall to hear the Mayor, Alderman Geoffrey Brown, read the proclamation of the accession of Queen Elizabeth II on 17 June 1952.

173 History merges with the present day as aldermen and councillors move through the town to the Old Town Hall where a guard of honour waits. The Queen's accession is proclaimed again in the traditional place where important public announcements have been made to the people of Godalming for 1,000 years.

174 Epilogue. Many of Godalming's historic and natural features appear in this 18th-century engraving which shows the famous first view of the town from the end of Meadrow. Although the hills were grazed, all early pictures show trees on the skyline, a feature which is still treasured today.

Select Bibliography

Bott, A., *Godalming Parish Church* (1987)

Brandon, P., *A History of Surrey* (1977)

Coombs, D. (edited for the Godalming Trust), *The Godalming 400* (1978), *A Godalming Walk* (1983), *Memories of Farncombe and Godalming* (1987)

Crocker, A. and G., *Catteshall Mill* (1981)

Crocker, G. (edited), *Industrial Archaeology of Surrey* (1990)

Dedman, S.C. (edited), *The Growth of a Town* —based on lectures by local historians using material from the Percy Woods manuscripts (1969)

Haveron, F., *The Brilliant Ray* (1981)

Haig-Brown, H., *Frith Hill Then and Now* (1990)

Head, R.E., *Godalming in old Picture Postcards* Vols. 1-3 (1984-94)

Janaway, J., *The Story of Godalming* (1983)

Janaway, J., *Yesterday's Town: Godalming* (1987)

Mayne, P.J., *Godalming Cricket, 225 Not Out* (1992)

Nyazai, M., *The Best Days of their Lives* (1994)

Pevsner, N., Nairn, I., Cherry, B., *The Buildings of England: Surrey* (1962)

Spalding, P. and Jackson, E., *James Edward Oglethorpe* (1988)

Stidder, D., *The Watermills of Surrey* (1990)

Waverley Borough Council, *Heritage Features in Waverley* (1986)

RAILWAY HOTEL,
OLD STATION,
GODALMING.
4 Miles from Guildford on the Portsmouth Road.

Luncheons, Dinners and Teas provided.

Good Accommodation for Cyclists and Tourists.
PARTIES PROVIDED FOR.

Wines & Spirits of the best quality.
Bass's Bottled Ales & Guinness's Stout.

M. EATON, *Proprietress.*

THE MUSEUM.

Visitors and others should call and see the Museum, which consists of Fowls, Dogs, Birds, Badgers, Fishes, Reptiles, Wild Cat, a Crocodile killed in the Common Meadows, a Wonderful "Cock-Hen," that Laid 300 Eggs, and a lot of other Curios found in the Neighbourhood, collected by the late Mr. Benjamin Battson over 40 years ago.